DUTCH OVEN COOKBOOK

FOR BEGINNERS

The Complete Step by Step and Easy to Follow Cookbook to Make Delicious, Restaurant Style and Affordable Dutch Cuisine Recipes at Home – A Treat for Beginner Cooks

Table of Contents

INTRODUCTION

Dutch ovens are round and hollow, weighty check cooking pots with tight-fitting covers that can be utilized either on a reach top or in the oven. The substantial metal or artistic development gives consistent, even, and multi-directional brilliant heat to the food being prepared inside. With a wide scope of employments, Dutch ovens are genuinely a generally useful piece of cookware.

All throughout the world
Dutch ovens, as they are brought in the United States today, have been utilized for many years, in a wide range of societies, and under numerous names. This most essential piece of cookware was initially planned with feet to sit above hot remains in a wood or coal consuming chimney. The tops of Dutch ovens were at one time slightly concave with the goal that hot coals could be set on top to give heat from above just as underneath. In France, these multi-use pots are known as cocottes, and in Brittan, they are referred to just as meals.

Employments

Present day Dutch ovens can be utilized on a burner like a stockpot or in the oven like a heating dish. The weighty check metal or earthenware can withstand a wide scope of temperatures and cooking strategies. Practically any cooking undertaking can be acted in a Dutch oven.

Soups and stews: Dutch ovens are ideal for soups and stews due to their size, shape, and thick development. The weighty metal or clay conducts heat well and can keep food warm for significant stretches of time. This is helpful for long-stewing soups, stews, or beans.

Simmering: When set inside an oven, Dutch ovens lead heat and move it to the food inside from all directions. The capacity of the cookware to hold this heat implies that less energy is needed for long, moderate cooking techniques. The ovenproof cover holds dampness and forestalls drying during long cooking times. This makes Dutch ovens ideal for moderate broiling meats or vegetables.

Dutch oven meals

15+ recipes

1. Dutch Oven Lasagna – Stove Top Lasagna

Prep: 15 minutes | Cook: 50 minutes | Total: 1 hour 5 minutes

Ingredients

- 9 oz. bundle no-bubble lasagna noodles
- 1 egg delicately beaten
- 1 15 oz. container ricotta cheddar or curds
- 1 tablespoon new minced parsley
- 1 lb. ground throw

- 1 lb. ground Italian hotdog
- 1 medium yellow onion diced
- 3 cloves garlic minced
- ½ cup dry or semi-dry red wine can supplant with water or chicken stock
- 1/8 teaspoon 2-3 runs red pepper chips
- 32-48 oz. marinara sauce your top pick
- 2 cups destroyed mozzarella cheddar or cuts of new mozzarella
- ½ cup ground Parmesan
- fresh basil harsh chopped

Directions

1. In a little bowl, beat together the egg, ricotta and parsley. Put in a safe spot.
2. In the Dutch oven, over medium-high warmth, earthy colored the meat and hotdog. Channel the meat holding 2 tablespoons fat (add 2 tablespoons olive oil, if there isn't sufficient saved fat). Move the drained meat to a huge, heatproof bowl and put in a safe spot.
3. In a similar pot, sauté the diced onion until it gets clear. Add the minced garlic and cook for an extra 30 seconds. Add red wine, red pepper chips and the marinara sauce and cook an

extra 5 minutes. Move the marinara blend to the bowl with the meat and blend to join.

4. With the Dutch oven over low-medium warmth, scoop 2 cups of the marinara meat blend into the lower part of the pot and cover the sauce with a layer of lasagna noodles (breaking the noodles to fit). At that point, spoon the noodles with a layer of the marinara meat blend.

5. Spot spoonful's of the ricotta/egg combination over the marinara blend and afterward adds some mozzarella and ground Parmesan. Rehash the layers three additional occasions (besides there will be just three layers with the ricotta blend).

6. The lasagna ought to be layered like this from the base layer to the top layer:

7. Marinara meat sauce, noodles, marinara meat sauce, ricotta blend, mozzarella, Parmesan, noodles, marinara, ricotta, mozzarella, Parmesan, noodles, marinara, ricotta, mozzarella, noodles, marinara, and mozzarella and get done with Parmesan.

8. Change warmth to low and cook, covered, 30-40 minutes or until the noodles are cooked

through, and the lasagna is hot and effervescent. At the point when the lasagna is cooked through and noodles have mellowed, it tends to be set under the grill for a couple of moments to brown the cheddar.

9. In the wake of eliminating the lasagna from the warmth, embellish it with new basil and let it rest 10-15 minutes prior to serving.

10. Appreciate!

2. Rich Pork Stew Recipe With Root Vegetables

PREP TIME: 30 minutes | COOK TIME: 1 hour |
TOTAL TIME: 1 hour 30 minutes

INGREDIENTS

- 2 1/2 lbs. boneless pork cook, cut into 1"
  shapes
- 1/4 cup universally handy flour
- 1/2 tsp. salt, separated
- 1/2 tsp. dark pepper, separated
- 1 tsp. smoked paprika
- 3 tbsp. olive oil

- 1 huge yellow onion, chopped
- 4 garlic cloves, minced
- 1 cup white wine (or chicken stock)
- 2 celery stems, cut into 1/2" pieces
- 5 carrots, stripped and cut into 1/2" pieces
- 4 medium Yukon gold potatoes, stripped and cut into 1" pieces
- 2 cups chicken stock
- 14.5 oz. can diced tomatoes
- 2 tbsp. Worcestershire sauce
- 2 cove leaves
- 1 tsp. dried basil
- 1/2 tsp. dried oregano
- 8 oz. Baby Bella mushrooms, chopped
- 1 cup frozen peas
- 1 pack parsley, chopped for embellish

Directions

1. Whisk together flour, 1/2 teaspoon salt, 1/2 teaspoon dark pepper, and paprika in a medium bowl at that point throw the pork shapes in it until covered; Coating pork in prepared flour
2. Warmth olive oil over medium warmth in an enormous Dutch oven;

3. When oil is hot, place the pork in an even layer on the lower part of the container. You may have to do this interaction in 2-3 clusters relying on the size of your Dutch oven and measure of pork utilized; Frying pork solid shapes in Dutch oven

4. Earthy colored the pork for 2-3 minutes on each side until all pieces are carmelized and afterward move to a plate;

5. Add the onion to the skillet and sauté for brief at that point add the garlic and cook for an additional 30 seconds blending as it cooks;

6. Add the wine or equivalent measures of stock to the Dutch oven and mix while scratching the lower part of the skillet to deglaze any cooked pieces from the pot;

7. Add the celery, carrots, potatoes, chicken stock, tomatoes, and Worcestershire sauce and mix to consolidate; Adding potatoes and tomatoes to Dutch oven

8. Add the sound leaves, dried basil, dried oregano, staying salt and dark pepper, at that point mix;

9. Heat the combination to the point of boiling, at that point lessen the warmth and stew for 45 minutes;
10. Add the pork back to the Dutch oven, mix and cover stewing for 30-40 minutes blending sporadically;
11. Add the mushrooms and frozen peas to the stew and stew revealed for an extra 10-15 minutes or until the mushrooms are delicate; Adding mushrooms and peas to pork stew
12. Season with extra salt and pepper if necessary, at that point present with a cut of bread and new parsley on top. Dutch oven of pork stew with metal ladel Pork stew in white bowl

NOTES

13. Serve this formula with a side of cornbread, rolls, or dry toasted bread.

3. Dutch Oven Tortellini Soup With Sausage

PREP TIME: 5 minutes | COOK TIME: 1 hour 30 minutes | TOTAL TIMEL: 1 hour 35 minutes

INGREDIENTS

- 1 lb Italian wiener, housings eliminated
- 2 tabs olive oil
- 1 onion, diced
- 4 cloves garlic, minced
- 5 cups hamburger stock
- 1 cup water
- 14 oz. can diced tomatoes
- 1 carrot, destroyed
- 1 tsp. dried basil

- 1/2 tsp. dried oregano
- 8 oz. would tomato be able to sauce
- 8 oz. new tortellini pasta
- 1 cup substantial cream
- 3 tbsp. chopped new parsley
- Trimmings
- New Basil, chopped
- Parsley, chopped
- Parmesan, ground

Directions

1. In a Dutch oven, heat oil over medium warmth and include the frankfurter at that point cook for 5-7 minutes; Frying wiener in Dutch oven
2. When the frankfurter has seared, eliminate and channel on a paper lined plate;
3. Dispose of everything except 1 tablespoon hotdog drippings from the dish;
4. Utilizing the hotdog drippings staying, sauté chopped onion and garlic over medium warmth for 3-4 minutes;
5. Mix in the hamburger stock, water, diced tomatoes, destroyed carrots, basil, oregano, pureed tomatoes, and drained hotdog; Pouring stock into Dutch oven

6. Heat this to the point of boiling, at that point diminish the warmth to low;

7. Stew revealed for 30 minutes;

8. At 30 minutes, skim any noticeable fat from the top and include the parsley at that point cover and cook for an extra 30 minutes;

9. Include the tortellini and cream at that point cook for an additional 10 minutes; Pouring tortellini in Dutch oven

10. Present with extra new parsley, new basil, and ground Parmesan cheddar. Wooden spoon of wiener tortellini soup Tortellini soup in white bowl

NOTES

11. Present with your number one hard bread.

4. Copycat Zuppa Toscana Soup Recipe

PREP TIME: 15 minutes | COOK TIME: 40 minutes |
TOTAL TIME: 55 minutes

INGREDIENTS

- 1 lb Italian frankfurter
- 8 cuts bacon, cut into little pieces
- 1 enormous onion, diced
- 2 tbsp. garlic, minced
- 1 cup carrots, chopped
- 8 cups chicken stock
- 6 potatoes, cubed
- 1 cup weighty cream

- 4 cups new infant spinach
- 1/2 tsp. salt
- 1 tsp. dark pepper

Guidelines

1. Over medium-high warmth, in a Dutch oven, cook the Italian hotdog until seared, not, at this point pink, and disintegrated well (around 10-12 minutes); Browning frankfurter
2. Eliminate the frankfurter from the Dutch oven and spot on a paper lined plate to deplete;
3. Add the bacon pieces to a similar Dutch oven and cook until fresh at that point put to the side on a paper lined plate to deplete;
4. Eliminate everything except 2 tablespoons of drippings from the Dutch oven;
5. To the Dutch oven, add the onions and garlic with the saved drippings and cook for 5 minutes;
6. Include the carrot pieces and keep cooking for an extra 5 minutes; Carrots in soup pot
7. Pour in the chicken stock, mix, and heat to the point of boiling over high warmth; Adding stock to soup pot

8. At the point when the blend reaches boiling point, include the diced potatoes and diminish the warmth to medium-high;

9. Cook the combination another 15-18 minutes until the potatoes are fork delicate;

10. Lessen the warmth to medium and mix in the hefty cream, bacon, and hotdog at that point bring back up to temperature being certain not to heat to the point of boiling, yet permit to stew; Pouring cream into soup pot

11. When the combination is stewing, add back in the spinach and eliminate from heat;

12. Put in a safe spot for 5-19 minutes prior to serving to permit the spinach to cook; Wooden spoon of zuppa Toscana soup

13. Present with a sprinkle of newly ground Parmesan cheddar and a side of bread or wafers. White bowl of zuppa Toscana soup

NOTES

14. Whenever liked, utilize chopped kale instead of spinach.

5. Slow-Cooked Chicken Stew with Kale

PREP TIME: 10 minutes | COOK TIME: 45 minutes | TOTAL TIME: 55 minutes

INGREDIENTS

Chicken Skin Gremolata:

- 8 pieces chicken thigh skin (saved from stew; see underneath)
- 1 little garlic clove, finely ground
- 2 Tbsp. finely chopped parsley
- 1 tsp. finely ground lemon zing
- Fit salt, newly ground pepper

Lemon Oil:

- 1 little lemon, ideally natural and unwaxed, meagerly sliced into adjusts, adjusts cut into quarters
- 1/3 cup extra-virgin olive oil
- Touch of sugar
- Legitimate salt, newly ground pepper

Stew and gathering:

- 4 lb. skin-on, bone-in chicken thighs (around 8), wiped off
- Legitimate salt, newly ground pepper
- 6 oz. bacon (around 6 cuts), chopped
- 4 huge shallots, quartered longwise
- 2 heads of garlic, split across
- 1/2 cup dry white wine
- 1 pack parsley, stems integrated with kitchen twine
- 2 inlet leaves
- 8 cups torn wavy kale leaves
- Daintily sliced radishes as well as meagerly sliced red onion (for serving; optional)

Arrangement

Chicken Skin Gremolata:

1. Preheat oven to 350°F. Orchestrate chicken skin in a solitary layer on a rimmed preparing sheet and heat until dull brilliant earthy colored

and fresh right through, 12–18 minutes. Let cool, at that point coarsely slash.

2. Consolidate chicken skin, garlic, parsley, and lemon zing in a little bowl; season with salt and pepper and throw to join.

Lemon Oil:

3. Consolidate lemon, olive oil, and sugar in a little bowl. Season with salt and pepper and let sit in any event 10 minutes, blending more than once.

Stew and gathering:

4. Season chicken thighs done with salt and pepper. Cook bacon in a huge Dutch oven or other substantial pot over medium-low warmth, mixing regularly, until earthy colored and fresh, 7–10 minutes. Utilizing an opened spoon, move bacon to a little bowl.

5. Increment warmth to medium-high. Working in 2 groups if necessary, cook chicken thighs, skin side down, in a similar pot until skin is brilliant earthy colored, 7–10 minutes. Move to a huge plate and turn skin side up. Eliminate pot from heat. Let chicken cool marginally, at that point pull skin from meat and move to a

shallow bowl; cover and chill (save for making the gremolata).

6. Return pot to medium warmth and cook shallots and garlic, cut side down, in a similar pot, throwing shallots periodically, until shallots are seared in spots and garlic is brilliant earthy colored, around 5 minutes. Add wine, blending to deliver any pieces stuck on the lower part of pot, and cook until diminished by 66%, around 2 minutes. Add parsley, sound leaves, held bacon, and 8 cups water, season liberally with salt and pepper, and bring to a stew. Return chicken thighs to pot and bring stew back up to a stew. Cover with a top, leaving marginally topsy-turvy so steam can get away, and cook, changing warmth to keep an extremely delicate stew and skimming froth from surface depending on the situation, until meat is delicate and effectively pulls from bones, 1/2 hours.

7. Move thighs to a cutting board and let cool 10–15 minutes; keep fluid at a stew. Pull meat from bones and attack scaled down pieces. Add bones back to pot as you go. Move meat to a medium bowl and cover with cling wrap. Add

kale and stew until kale is delicate and fluid is extremely tasty, 25–30 minutes.

8. Eliminate stew from heat, add meat back to pot, and let cool revealed (bones and all) until done steaming. Cover pot and chill stew in any event 12 hours (you can avoid this progression, yet it will significantly improve the flavor).

9. Uncover stew and spoon off half to 3/4 of fat on a superficial level; dispose of. Delicately warm stew until scarcely stewing. Pluck out and dispose of bones, parsley, and straight leaves. Taste and season with more salt and pepper if necessary. Spoon stew into bowls and top as wanted.

10. Do Ahead

11. Lemon oil can be made 2 days ahead. Cover and chill. Bring to room temperature prior to utilizing.

12. Stew can be made 3 days ahead. Keep chilled.

6. Warm-Spiced Saucy Lamb Stew

PREP TIME: 40 minutes | COOK TIME: 30 minutes | TOTAL TIME: 1 hour 10 minutes

INGREDIENTS

Toasted Cauliflower Crumbs:

- 1/2 medium head of cauliflower
- 3 Tbsp. extra-virgin olive oil
- Legitimate salt, newly ground pepper

Lemony Mint Yogurt:

- 1 cup plain entire milk Greek yogurt

- 3 Tbsp. finely chopped mint
- 1 Tbsp. new lemon juice
- Genuine salt, newly ground pepper

Stew and gathering:

- 5 lb. sheep shanks (around 6), wiped off
- Genuine salt, newly ground pepper
- 1/4 cup extra-virgin olive oil
- 2 huge red onions, cut into 1" wedges
- 2 heads of garlic, split transversely
- 1 (3") stick cinnamon or 1/2 tsp. ground cinnamon
- 1/2 tsp. coriander seeds, squashed
- 3 Tbsp. harissa glue
- Torn pitted Castelvetrano olives, mint leaves, or potentially finely chopped saved lemon (for serving; optional)

Readiness

Toasted Cauliflower Crumbs:

1. Coarsely cleave cauliflower and heartbeat in a food processor until about the size of grains of rice (or, you can finely slash with a blade all things being equal). You ought to have around 2 cups.

2. Warmth oil in an enormous skillet, ideally cast iron, over medium-high. Cook cauliflower,

blending frequently, until brilliant earthy colored all finished and scorched in spots, 6–8 minutes. Eliminate from heat; season with salt and pepper. Give cool access skillet.

Lemony Mint Yogurt:

3. Blend yogurt, mint, and lemon juice in a medium bowl; season with salt and pepper.

Stew and gathering:

4. Season sheep shanks liberally done with salt and pepper. Warmth oil in an enormous Dutch oven or other substantial pot over medium-high. Working in 2 bunches, cook sheep shanks in a solitary layer, turning at times, until carmelized all more than, 8–12 minutes for each group. As the shanks get done with cooking, move to an enormous plate.

5. Decrease warmth to medium; add onions and garlic, cut side down, to a similar pot and cook, throwing onions infrequently, until onions are carmelized in spots and garlic is brilliant earthy colored, around 5 minutes. Add cinnamon and squashed coriander and cook, mixing continually, until flavors are fragrant, around 1 moment. Add harissa glue and cook, mixing regularly and scratching lower part of pot, until

vegetables are covered and glue is marginally obscured in shading, around 2 minutes. Add 7 cups water, mixing to deliver any pieces stuck on lower part of pot. Season liberally with salt and pepper and bring to a stew. Return sheep shanks to pot and bring stew back up to a stew. Cover with a top, leaving marginally to one side so steam can get away, and cook, changing warmth to keep a delicate stew and skimming froth from surface on a case by case basis, until meat is delicate and effectively pulls from bones, 1/2–2 hours.

6. Move sheep shanks to a cutting board and let cool 10–15 minutes; keep fluid at a stew. Pull meat from bones and attack scaled down pieces. Add bones back to pot as you go. Move meat to a medium bowl and cover with saran wrap.

7. Stew bones in stock, uncovered, until fluid is thick and tasty, 25–30 minutes. Eliminate from heat; add meat back to pot and let cool uncovered (bones and all) until done steaming. Cover pot and chill stew in any event 12 hours (you can skirt this progression, yet it will drastically improve the flavor).

8. Reveal stew and spoon off half to 3/4 of fat on a superficial level; dispose of. Tenderly warm stew until scarcely stewing. Pluck out and dispose of bones. Taste and season with more salt and pepper if necessary. Spoon stew into bowls and present with Toasted Cauliflower Crumbs, Mint Yogurt, harissa, and olives, mint leaves, and additionally safeguarded lemon as wanted.

9. Do Ahead

10. Yogurt can be made 1 day ahead. Cover and chill.

11. Stew can be made 3 days ahead. Keep chilled

7. Instant Pot Lamb Haleem

YIELD4–6 Servings | ACTIVE TIME 50 minutes|
TOTAL TIME5½ to 20 hours

INGREDIENTS

- ¾ cup arranged dals, (for example, chana dal, moong dal, masoor dal, and additionally urad dal)
- ¼ cup white jasmine rice or other long-grain rice
- ¼ cup pearl grain
- 1½ lb. bone-in sheep stew meat
- 3 tsp. fit salt, isolated, in addition to additional
- 1 6" piece new ginger

- 3 medium shallots, meagerly sliced
- ⅓ cup ghee or vegetable oil
- 4 garlic cloves, finely ground
- 2 Tbsp. furthermore 1½ tsp. garam masala
- 1 tsp. (or then again more) cayenne pepper
- 1 tsp. ground turmeric
- 3 green Thai chilies, stems eliminated (optional)
- ½ cup (softly pressed) chopped cilantro, in addition to additional for serving
- ½ white onion, finely chopped
- 2 limes, cut into wedges

Readiness

1. Join dals, rice, and grain in a medium bowl. Pour in water to cover and wash dals and grains around with your fingers. Channel and rehash measure until water runs adequately clear to own your hands. Pour in water to cover and let dals and grains splash at room temperature in any event 2 hours, or cover and chill as long as 12 hours.

2. Spot sheep on a plate, wipe off with paper towels, and season done with 2 tsp. salt; put in a safe spot. Strip ginger by scratching off skin with a spoon. Finely grind half of ginger; put in

a safe spot. Meagerly cut excess ginger. Stack cuts and cut across into matchsticks; put in a safe spot.

3. On the off chance that utilizing an electric pressing factor cooker, join shallots and ghee in pot and set to sauté capacity or high. Cook, blending regularly and changing warmth on a case by case basis if your cooker has that alternative, until shallots are simply starting to brown, around 8 minutes (or around 6 minutes if cooking in oil). Diminish to typical capacity or medium if conceivable, or, if your cooker doesn't have a lower setting, turn off briefly if blend is getting excessively hot. Add held ginger matchsticks and cook, mixing regularly, until shallots are earthy colored and fresh and ginger is frizzled, 4–10 minutes, contingent upon your cooker. Utilizing an opened spoon, move shallots and ginger to a plate, fanning out into a solitary layer. Season daintily with salt; let cool.

4. Add garlic, garam masala, cayenne, turmeric, and held ground ginger, and cook, blending continually, until fragrant, around 30 seconds. Add sheep and mix to cover in flavors. Cook,

mixing frequently with a wooden spoon and over and again adding sprinkles of water as flavors stick to lower part of pot and scraping up carmelized bits, until flavors meet up, around 15 minutes. (Bhuna, the interaction of continued staying and scratching, is a Southeast Asian cooking procedure that draws out the kind of the flavors and guarantees they don't taste crude and grainy.)

5. Channel dal combination and add to pot alongside 1 tsp. salt and 5 cups water. Secure cover and bring to full pressing factor as per producer's bearings. Cook 1½ hours. Let sit 20 minutes, at that point physically discharge pressing factor and open up.

6. Taste haleem and add more salt and cayenne if necessary. Add chilies if utilizing. (These are for flavor, not warmth; don't hesitate to forget about them.) Simmer on ordinary capacity or medium, mixing frequently, 5 minutes. Mix in ½ cup cilantro.

7. Serve haleem with white onion, lime wedges, saved firm shallots and ginger, and more chopped cilantro.

8. In the event that utilizing a medium Dutch oven or burner pressure cooker, cook shallots and ghee over high warmth, mixing frequently, until shallots are simply starting to brown, around 8 minutes (or around 6 minutes if cooking in oil). Add held ginger matchsticks and cook, blending frequently, until shallots are earthy colored and fresh and ginger is frizzled, 5–8 minutes. Utilizing an opened spoon, move shallots and ginger to a plate, fanning out in a solitary layer. Season gently with salt; let cool.

9. Decrease warmth to medium, add garlic, garam masala, cayenne, turmeric, and saved ground ginger, and cook, blending continually, until fragrant, around 30 seconds. Add sheep and mix to cover in flavors. Cook, mixing frequently with a wooden spoon and more than once adding sprinkles of water as flavors stick to lower part of pot and scraping up sautéed bits, until flavors meet up, around 15 minutes. (Bhuna, the interaction of continued staying and scratching, is a Southeast Asian cooking method that draws out the kind of the flavors

and guarantees they don't taste crude and grainy.)

10. Channel dal blend and add to pot alongside 1 tsp. salt and 6½ cups water (if utilizing a Dutch oven) or 5 cups water (for pressure cooker). Increment warmth to high and heat to the point of boiling, at that point decrease warmth to the low, cover pot, and cook, mixing and scratching lower part of pot each 15–20 minutes, until meat is tumbling off the bone and dals and grains have almost dissolved into the stew, 4½–5 hours. (In the event that utilizing a burner cooker, increment warmth to high and heat to the point of boiling. Secure cover and bring to full pressing factor as indicated by maker's headings. Cook 1½ hours. Let sit 20 minutes, at that point physically discharge pressing factor and open up.)

11. Taste haleem and add more salt and cayenne if necessary. Add chilies if utilizing. (These are for flavor, not warmth; don't hesitate to forget about them.) Simmer over medium warmth, mixing regularly, 5 minutes. Mix in ½ cup cilantro.

12. Serve haleem with white onion, lime wedges, saved fresh shallots and ginger, and more chopped cilantro.
13. Do ahead: Haleem can be made 1 day ahead. Let cool; cover and chill. Warm over medium until warmed through.

8. Braised Duck Legs With Polenta And Wilted Chard

PREP TIME: 25 minutes| COOK TIME: 55 minutes|
TOTAL TIME: 1 hour 20 minutes

INGREDIENTS

- For the duck:
- 4 pounds duck legs
- Genuine salt, newly ground pepper
- 12 branches thyme
- 10 cloves garlic, squashed
- 2 straight leaves, disintegrated
- 2 teaspoons juniper berries
- 1 tablespoon vegetable oil

- 1 huge onion, chopped
- 2 medium carrots, stripped, chopped
- 2 stems celery, chopped
- 1/2 cups dry red wine
- For the polenta:
- 1/2 cups milk
- Genuine salt, newly ground pepper
- 2/3 cup coarse-crush polenta
- For the gathering:
- 1 teaspoon Sherry vinegar or red wine vinegar
- 1 bundle huge Swiss chard
- 3 tablespoons olive oil, partitioned
- 6 cloves garlic, squashed
- Genuine salt, newly ground pepper
- 1/2 teaspoon squashed red pepper pieces
- 1 lemon, split
- 1 ounce Parmesan, finely ground (around 1 cup)
- 2 tablespoons unsalted margarine

Readiness

For the duck:

1. Prick duck skin done with a paring blade or cutting fork; season with salt and pepper. Spot duck on an enormous rimmed heating sheet. Throw with thyme, garlic, inlet leaves, and

juniper berries, squeezing aromatics onto legs to follow. Let sit 30 minutes (or ideally do this the other day; cover and chill).

2. Spot racks in upper and lower thirds of oven and preheat to 225°F. Warmth oil in an enormous Dutch oven or other hefty pot over medium and cook onion, carrots, and celery, blending at times, until mellowed, 8–10 minutes. Add wine, heat to the point of boiling, and cook until diminished considerably, 6–8 minutes. Add 1 cup water and slip duck legs (counting aromatics), skin side down, into fluid. Cover and braise in oven on lower rack until duck is lowered in its fat, 1/2–2 hours. Turn duck skin side up and cook, covered, until delicate (the bones will squirm effectively in the joint), 1/2–2 hours longer.

3. Move duck to a profound preparing dish; strain fluid into an enormous estimating glass or medium bowl. Skim fat into dish with duck; put to the side braising juices. Chill duck, in any event 1 hour and as long as 2 days (cover and chill juices if chilling duck in excess several hours).

4. For the polenta:

5. While duck is chilling, preheat oven to 225°F. Heat milk and 2 cups water to the point of boiling in a huge pot. Season with salt and pepper; gradually stream in polenta, whisking continually. Cook, whisking frequently, until it starts to thicken, around 5 minutes. Cover and move to bring down rack in oven. Heat until polenta is thick and grains are delicate, 20–30 minutes. Rush to streamline.

6. For the gathering:

7. While the polenta is in the oven, heat saved braising juices to the point of boiling in a medium skillet over medium-high warmth and cook until adequately thick to cover a spoon, 15–20 minutes. Mix in vinegar; keep sauce warm.

8. Eliminate polenta from oven; keep warm. Increment oven temperature to 400°F. Move duck legs, abandoning fat, to a huge rimmed heating sheet, putting skin side up. Cook on top rack until skin is popping fresh, around 20 minutes.

9. In the interim, eliminate ribs and comes from chard leaves by cutting away leaf from the two

sides of tail. Cut tail fifty-fifty longwise; cut into 3"- long pieces. Tear leaves. Warmth half of oil in a huge skillet over medium-high. Cook garlic, throwing, until brilliant, around 2 minutes. Move to a huge bowl. Add stems to skillet and cook, throwing, until fresh delicate, around 5 minutes. Move to bowl with garlic.

10. Add remaining oil to skillet; add chard leaves a modest bunch at a time, letting them shrivel marginally prior to adding more, and cook, throwing, until chard is simply withered, around 2 minutes. Season with salt and pepper. Throw in chard stems and garlic and move to a platter. Top with red pepper pieces and crush lemon over.

11. Whisk Parmesan and spread into polenta. Serve duck with polenta, withered chard, and sauce close by.

9.   Dutch Oven Bread

Prep time: 10 minutes | cook time: 1 hour|
additional time: 2 hours| total time: 3 hours 10
minutes

INGREDIENTS

- 1/2 cup warm milk 125 ml (you may utilize water in the event that you don't have milk)
- 1/4 teaspoon sugar (1g)
- 1 pack dry dynamic yeast, around 2 teaspoons
- 4 cups All-Purpose Flour + some for cleaning (500g)
- 3/4 tablespoon salt (15-17g)
- 1 cup Lukewarm water add a sprinkle extra if necessary (236 ml)

- 1 egg, blended
- 1 tablespoon Olive Oil + for lubing

Directions

1. The Best Dutch Oven Bread
2. Mix yeast bundle into a warm to contact milk and sugar and permit the yeast to sprout for around 5 minutes. At the point when it begins to air pocket and froth, it implies the yeast is dynamic and fit to be utilized.
3. In an enormous bowl, blend flour and salt, at that point make a little well in the center and pour in the milk and yeast combination.
4. Blend one egg in with warm water to heat up chilly egg, and add to the flour.
5. Utilizing your wooden spoon or spatula, begin joining everything. When consolidated utilizing your hands, start to manipulate the batter; when it begins to pull away from the sides of the bowl, it is prepared to rest. I work for around 5 minutes. On the off chance that the mixture is excessively tacky, add more, a few tablespoons all at once, and the other way around, add a sprinkle more water if it's excessively dry—shower olive oil and tap/coat everywhere on the batter.

6. Cover the bowl with a huge kitchen towel and let it ascend until it pairs in size. It requires a little while hours, at times less if the house is hotter. (RISE 1)

7. Uncover the batter and give it a couple of jabs with your finger. In the event that the batter has risen appropriately, it should indent under the tension of your fingers and gradually collapse. Now, you could put the mixture in the preparing skillet, yet following stage 7. the bread turns out such a ton better.

8. Utilizing your hand, overlap the mixture—light pressing factor manipulating. Add more flour until it meets up. Cover and let it ascend for one more hour. You may surrender it for to 3 hours. You don't need to sit tight for the second ascent however the bread turned out so great. (RISE 2-optional). Assuming you decide not to do this subsequent ascent, simply move to stage 10.

9. Preheat the oven to 450 F

10. When the mixture has multiplied by and by, manipulate it again to shape it.

11. Spot the molded mixture into a gently lubed or material lined Dutch oven, and let it ascend for

the second time at the hotter territory.
Sprinkle the top with a touch of flour and score lines on top. As the bread heats, it will extend, and those scored lines will turn out to be more noticeable. (RISE 3)

12. Likewise, you could preheat the plated Dutch oven prior to preparing by showering a touch of oil first. At that point place it in the cool oven to warm up bit by bit for around 10 minutes or something like that. Never put a chilly, void pot in a hot oven to warm. So heat Dutch oven for somewhat first at that point, place the mixture in. This technique will keep Dutch oven from breaking. You can likewise warm it on the burner. Whichever step you take, it will be fine. In case you're concerned, the most secure bet is to utilize a non-plated and clay Dutch oven when heating bread.

13. Prepare for around 45 to 50 minutes, eliminating the cover totally 8-10 minutes before the bread is finished. Thusly, it will get a more profound tone and crispier.

14. Eliminate bread from a Dutch oven, envelop it by the kitchen towel and let it cool for in any event 30 minutes prior to cutting. Trust me on

this one. In the event that you cut it when the bread is hot, it will get tacky inside, so better sit tight for only a tad.

15. NOTES

16. You may skirt the egg.

17. You may utilize water rather than milk.

18. The result of the bread relies upon the water temperature, oven, flour, yeast even air. This formula is tried and retested ordinarily.

19. You may preheat your Dutch oven or you can really make it in the standard preparing dish. You don't need to utilize material paper, yet I like utilizing it.

20. Try not to quit preparing if the bread doesn't come out amazing the first run through... like I said it very well may be a wide range of things to influence it.

21. In the event that you going to make bigger bread, add 6 cups of flour, 1 tablespoon Salt and enough fluid to make it sufficiently wet. I would say around 2 1/2 cups. All the other things are something very similar.

22. More slender or softer (with a bit more water) dough in a warm kitchen will probably rise in 45 minutes or less.

23. Firmer dough with less moisture will take longer to rise. Yeast is very sensitive to temperature; even a few degrees less in the kitchen can extend the rise time significantly.

24. On the off chance that your Dutch oven is too big and does not fit in the middle oven rack, instead you have to keep it at the bottom or lower rack, turn down the heat. It will still bake no worries. This will at least prevent burning. You can also add some parchment paper at the bottom just to make sure.

10. Kale and Cannellini Bean Stew

Prep time: 30 minutes| cook time: 1 hour| additional
time: 1 hours| total time: 2 hours 30 minutes

INGREDIENTS
For the Parmesan-garlic stock:

- 2 tablespoons olive oil
- 1 enormous onion, chopped
- 2 enormous heads garlic, cloves squashed and stripped
- Squeeze fit salt
- 8 cups (2 quarts) low-sodium chicken stock or stock, brilliant vegetable stock, or water

- 4 enormous new thyme branches
- 4 enormous new sage branches
- 12 level leaf new parsley branches
- 1 teaspoon entire dark peppercorns
- 1 teaspoon pickling zest (or 1 inlet leaf, 4 entire allspice berries, 4 entire cloves, and squeeze coriander seeds)
- 1 cup dry white wine
- 1 pound Parmesan cheddar skins

For the stew:
- 2 tablespoons olive oil, in addition to additional for the bread
- 1 enormous onion, diced (around 2 1/2 cups)
- 2 medium carrots, diced (around 1 cup)
- 2 medium celery stems, diced (around 1 cup)
- 3 enormous garlic cloves, meagerly sliced
- Fit salt
- 3 (5-ounce) bundles infant kale, or 1 pack level leaf kale, stems disposed of and leaves destroyed
- 1 (15-ounce) can dainty diced tomatoes with their juices
- 4 (15-ounce) jars cannellini beans, drained
- 1/4 cup sherry or red wine vinegar
- Newly ground dark pepper

- Red pepper drops
- 8 thick cuts dry bread
- Shaved Parmesan cheddar

Guidelines

Make the stock:

1. Warmth the oil in an enormous pot or little pot over medium-high warmth until sparkling. Add the onion, garlic, and salt, and mix to cover. Cook, blending regularly, until delicate and brilliant earthy colored, around 15 minutes.

2. Mix in the thyme, sage, parsley, peppercorns, and pickling zest, and cook 1 moment while blending. Add the wine and scrape up any cooked pieces from the lower part of the pot. Stew until decreased considerably, around 5 minutes.

3. Mix in the stock or water and Parmesan skins. Heat to the point of boiling. Lessen the warmth to low, at that point stew until the fluid decreases considerably, around 2 hours.

4. Strain through a fine sifter into a huge bowl, pushing on the solids. Dispose of the solids (albeit a few groups can't avoid scratching the mollified cheddar from the skins for a cook's treat). You ought to have around 4 cups (on

the off chance that you are short, add water to get to 4 cups). Use inside 60 minutes, or cool to room temperature, cover, and refrigerate for as long as 3 days or freeze in a water/air proof compartment for as long as 3 months. Whenever refrigerated or frozen, let come to room temperature prior to utilizing.

Make the stew:

1. Organize a rack in the oven and warmth the grill. Warmth the oil in a huge pot or Dutch oven over medium-high warmth until shining. Mix in the onion, carrots, celery, garlic, and a major spot of salt, and mix to cover. Cook, mixing once in a while, until delicate, around 10 minutes.

2. Add the kale a major modest bunch at a time, stirring to shrink prior to adding more. Mix in the held Parmesan stock, tomatoes, beans, and another spot of salt. Stew until the kale is delicate and the beans have lost their canned taste, around 15 minutes. Mix in the vinegar and season liberally with salt, pepper, and pepper chips. Keep warm over exceptionally low warmth.

3. Brush the two sides of the bread with olive oil and sprinkle with salt and pepper. Orchestrate in a solitary layer on a heating sheet. Cook until seared on top, around 3 minutes. Flip the bread and cover the opposite side of the bread with Parmesan twists. Sear until the edges of the bread are fresh and the cheddar is sautéed and effervescent, around 5 minutes more. Spot a cut in each serving bowl and scoop in the stew. Serve hot.

Formula Notes

1. Make ahead: The cooled stock can be put away in an impenetrable compartment in the cooler for as long as 3 days or frozen for as long as 3 months.
2. Capacity: Leftovers can be put away in an impenetrable compartment in the cooler for as long as 5 days.

11. Lamb Bolognese

Prep time: 5 minutes | additional time: 1 hours| total
time: 1 hour 10 minutes

INGREDIENTS

For the sauce:

- 2 tablespoons vegetable oil
- 1 pound ground sheep (75% lean/25% fat)
- Fit salt
- 1/2 cup finely chopped yellow onion
- 1/4 cup finely chopped carrots
- 1/4 cup finely chopped celery
- 1/2 teaspoon ground cumin
- 1/2 teaspoon ground coriander
- 3 cloves garlic, minced
- 2 cups dry red wine

- 1 cup diced tomatoes, ideally San Marzano
- 1 cup low-sodium chicken stock
- 1/3 cup weighty cream
- 2 narrows leaves
- 1 cinnamon stick
- 1 squeeze red pepper drops
- 1 squeeze granulated sugar (optional)

For the pasta:

- 2 pounds dry tagliatelle or pappardelle pasta
- 1 cup coarsely chopped new parsley leaves
- 1 cup coarsely chopped new mint leaves
- 1/3 cup ground Pecorino Romano or Parmesan cheddar
- 2 tablespoons extra-virgin olive oil

Guidelines

1. For the sauce: Heat the oil in a Dutch oven over medium-high warmth until simply beginning to smoke. Add the sheep and a liberal spot of salt and cook, blending at times, until seared, 4 to 5 minutes.

2. Add the onion, carrots, celery, cumin, coriander, and another great spot of salt to the seared sheep and keep cooking until the vegetables are clear and fragrant, 3 to 4

minutes. Add the garlic and cook for one more moment.

3. Add the wine and deglaze the skillet, trying to scratch the base with a wooden spoon to deliver the seared pieces. Stew the wine until it decreases significantly.

4. Add the tomatoes, chicken stock, cream, cove leaves, cinnamon, and red pepper drops. Lessen the warmth to medium-low and stew for 30 to 40 minutes. Taste your sauce irregularly and add salt if necessary. In the event that you track down that the sauce is turning into all in all too acidic, add a spot of sugar, as it will help balance the flavors.

5. While the sauce is stewing, heat an enormous pot of liberally salted water to the point of boiling. Taste your water. It should possess a flavor like ocean water.

6. For the pasta: When you have around 10 minutes left for the sauce to cook, add the pasta to the water and cook until still somewhat firm. (In the event that you have any worries about cooking times with dry pasta, read the bundling. The producer's

bearings are generally lovely right on the money.)

7. Save 1/2 cup of the pasta cooking water, at that point channel the pasta. Add the pasta into the pot of sauce and mix to join. Add the held pasta water, spices, cheddar, and olive oil and mix to join. When everything is fused and the sauce has started to thicken and cover the pasta, eliminate from the warmth and serve.

Formula Notes

1. Food processor prep: You can finely slash the onions, celery, and carrots together in a food processor in the event that you decide.

12. Braised Short Ribs

YIELDS: 4 servings | PREP TIME: 0 hours 20 mins
|COOK TIME: 2 hours 0 mins| TOTAL TIME: 2 hours
20 mins

INGREDIENTS

- 3 pounds bone-in meat short ribs
- 2 tablespoons vegetable or high smoking point oil
- Salt
- Newly ground dark pepper
- 1 huge onion, sliced
- 4 cloves garlic, minced

- 3 cups fluid, like brew, wine, or low-sodium stock
- 2 to 4 twigs new spices, like rosemary or thyme

Gear

- Cake or seasoning brush
- Dutch oven or profound sauté dish with a top

Directions

1. Warmth the oven and season the meat. Mastermind a rack in the lower third of the oven; eliminate the racks above it, and warmth to 325°F. Brush each short rib with the oil; at that point sprinkle liberally with salt and pepper.

2. Earthy colored the short ribs. Warmth a profound, wide Dutch oven or sauté dish over medium-high warmth. Add the short ribs in a single layer, leaving room among each and working in clusters if fundamental. Presently would be a decent second to turn on your hood vent or fan, on the off chance that you have one! Burn the short ribs without moving for a few minutes on each side, allowing them to brown profoundly. Use utensils to turn and

burn all sides. This will require around 15 minutes absolute.

3. Cook the onions. Turn the warmth down to medium and add the onion and garlic around the seared short ribs. Allow the onions to cook until they mollify, around 5 minutes.

4. Add fluid. Add the fluid — lager, wine, or stock — and bring to a stew.

5. Braise in the oven. After the fluid goes to a stew, add the spice twigs. Cover and spot in the oven. (Then again, this is where you can move to the sluggish cooker for 8 hours on the LOW setting, or keep cooking on extremely low warmth on the burner.) Braise in the oven until the meat is exceptionally delicate and pulling away from the bone, 2 to 2 1/2 hours.

6. Rest the meat. At the point when the meat is done, rest in a covered search for gold minutes prior to serving. Serve by tenderly pulling the pieces of meat away from the bone and spooning the sassy onions up and over.

7. OPTIONAL STEP — Refrigerate for the time being. While short ribs can be served quickly, they are a greasy cut, which makes the dish exceptionally rich and surprisingly oily. I like to

allow the ribs to sit in the sauce and cool to room temperature, at that point cover and refrigerate them short-term. Now, you can scratch away the solidified layer of fat from the top prior to warming. They will likewise improve in flavor and delicacy while resting for the time being.

8. Warm. To warm, cover and warm over low warmth on the oven for 15 to 20 minutes.

9. Formula NOTES

10. Moderate cooker guidelines: To cook in the sluggish cooker, progress through stage 4, at that point move the meat, onions, and fluid to a lethargic cooker embed. Cook on the LOW setting for 8 hours.

11. Burner guidelines: Instead of moving the container to the oven, you can likewise cook the short ribs on the burner. Keep the dish covered and cook over low warmth for 2 to 3 hours, checking fluid levels irregularly and ensuring the base isn't singing.

12. Flavor varieties: This is obviously the most essential strategy. You can get innovative by utilizing a flavor rub, various types of brew (I like the slight sharpness an IPA gives) or red

wine, or sherry. You can utilize a sprinkle of soy sauce and mirin with Chinese five-flavor; you could go Spanish with smoked paprika and Rioja.

13. Capacity: Leftovers can be put away in a hermetically sealed compartment in the cooler for as long as 4 days or frozen for as long as 3 months

13. Dutch Oven Braised Turkey

Prep Time 20 minutes| Cook Time 2 hours| Total Time 2 hours 20 minutes

INGREDIENTS

- 2 skin-on, bone-in turkey drumsticks (1/2 to 2 pounds complete)
- 2 skin-on, bone-in turkey thighs (around 3 pounds complete)
- Genuine salt
- Newly ground dark pepper
- 1 tablespoon olive oil
- 1/4 pound pancetta or bacon, slice to 1/2-inch pieces

- 2 leeks, white and light green parts, daintily sliced
- 2 medium celery stems, coarsely chopped
- 3 cloves garlic, minced
- 3/4 cup dry white wine
- 6 twigs new thyme
- 1/4 cup coarsely chopped new sage leaves
- 2 sound leaves
- 2 cups turkey or chicken stock
- 1 huge bundle collard greens, focus ribs eliminated, leaves chopped (around 6 cups chopped)
- 3 medium yams, stripped and cut into 2-inch 3D squares
- 2 tablespoons apple juice vinegar

Guidelines

1. Mastermind a rack in the oven and warmth to 350°F.
2. Pat the turkey pieces totally dry with paper towels. Liberally season the meat done with salt and pepper.
3. Warmth the oil in an enormous Dutch oven over high warmth until gleaming. Add the turkey skin-side down without swarming the

pot and working in bunches if vital. Burn each side until profoundly sautéed, 4 to 5 minutes for every side. Move to a plate; put in a safe spot.

4. Lower the warmth to medium and add the pancetta or bacon. Cook, mixing incidentally, until the fat is delivered and the meat is very much seared. Mix in the leeks and celery, season with 1/2 teaspoon salt and pepper, and cook until mollified, 6 to 8 minutes. Add the garlic and cook briefly more.

5. Add the wine and go through a wooden spoon to scratch any carmelized bits from the base. Cook until the wine is diminished by about half. Add the thyme, savvy, narrows leaves, and stock to the pot, at that point heat to the point of boiling. Add the collard greens and lower them in the fluid however much as could be expected (they won't be completely lowered). Spot the turkey pieces skin-side up on top of the greens.

6. Prepare revealed for 60 minutes. Mix in the yams, keeping the turkey skin uncovered. Return the pot to the oven and prepare until the meat is cooked through and registers an

inward temperature of 165°F, around 1 hour more.

7. Mix in the apple juice vinegar. Allow them to braise represent in any event 5 minutes prior to serving.

8. Formula NOTES

9. Capacity: Leftovers can be put away in an impermeable compartment in the cooler for as long as 5 days, or in the cooler for as long as 3 months.

14. Chicken in Coconut Milk with Lemongrass

Total: 55 min| Prep: 10 min| Cook: 45 min| Yield: 4 servings

INGREDIENTS

- 1 entire simmering chicken (3 to 4 pounds)
- Ocean salt and newly ground dark pepper
- 4 tablespoons (1/2 stick) margarine
- 1 tablespoon olive oil
- 1 cinnamon stick
- 2 entire star anise
- 1/2 cup generally chopped cilantro stems
- 1 enormous lemon, cut into eighths

- 1 tail lemongrass, 5 crawls of white part in particular, chopped into 1/4-inch pieces
- 6 to 8 cloves garlic, stripped and crushed
- 1 (14-to 16-ounce) would coconut be able to drain
- 3 cups torn greens (spinach, kale, chard, mizuna, and so forth)
- 2 green onions, chopped into 1/4-inch pieces
- Chopped cilantro, to decorate
- Cooked rice, to serve

Guidelines

1. Wipe the chicken off and sprinkle it generously with salt and pepper. Put the chicken, covered, in the fridge for as long as 24 hours, or in case you will cook it immediately, put it in a safe spot while you get ready leftover ingredients.
2. At the point when prepared to heat the chicken, preheat the oven to 375°F.
3. Soften the spread in a huge Dutch oven over medium warmth; at that point add the oil. Put in the chicken, bosom side up, and let it sizzle for around 30 seconds. Cautiously flip the bird and fresh the opposite side for an additional 30 seconds. Eliminate the container from the

warmth, put the chicken on a plate, and pour off the fat in the pot.

4. Move the chicken back into the pot, bosom side up, and add the cinnamon stick, star anise, chopped cilantro stems, lemon, lemongrass, garlic, and coconut milk. Cook, uncovered, in the preheated oven for 60 to an hour and a half (contingent upon size). Spoon the sauce over the highest point of the bird to treat at regular intervals or something like that. The chicken is done when a moment read thermometer embedded into the thigh peruses 165°F.

5. Eliminate chicken from the pot and put it on a plate. Pull out and dispose of the cinnamon stick and star anise. Set the pot with the sauce back on the burner over medium warmth, add the spinach and mix until just shriveled, around 10 seconds.

6. Cut the chicken and serve each piece over rice with sauce spooned over the top. Enhancement with chopped scallions and cilantro leaves.

15. Bone Broth on the Stove

Yield: 4 QUART| Prep time: 30 MINUTES | Cook time: 3 HOURS | Total time: 3 HOURS 30 MINUTES

INGREDIENTS

- 2 pounds blended meat bones, short ribs, oxtails, knuckles, and neck bones (see Recipe Note)
- 3 quarts separated water, in addition to additional on a case by case basis to cover
- 2 tablespoons apple juice vinegar
- 1 huge carrot
- 1 huge yellow onion

Gear

- Huge stockpot or 6-quart or bigger sluggish cooker
- Cheesecloth (optional)

Directions

Burner Instructions

1. Preheat the oven to 400°F and wash the bones. Orchestrate a rack in the oven and warmth to 400°F. Spot the bones in a colander, wash under cool water, and wipe off with paper towels.

2. Cook the bones for 30 minutes. Organize the bones in a solitary layer on a rimmed heating sheet. Cook until brilliant earthy colored, around 30 minutes.

3. Cover the bones with water and the vinegar and rest for 30 minutes. Move the hot issues that remain to be worked out enormous stockpot. Add the water and vinegar and mix to join. Cover and let sit for 30 minutes.

4. Carry the pot to a stew over high warmth. Carry the water to a fast stew over high warmth.

5. Skim the stock for the principal hour. Quickly turn the warmth down to the most reduced

setting conceivable. Check the pot at times, skimming off any froth that gathers on a superficial level and adding extra water depending on the situation to keep the ingredients covered. Cover and save the stock at a low stew for 24 hours.

6. Add the onions and carrots and cook for another 12 to 24 hours. Add the carrots and onions and keep on stewing for 12 to 24 hours more, adding more separated water on a case by case basis to keep the bones covered. The stock is done when it is a rich brilliant earthy colored and the bones are self-destructing at the joints.

7. Strain the bone stock. At the point when the stock is done, strain and cool the bone stock as fast as could really be expected. Set a sifter over an enormous pot or even a stand blender bowl and line it with cheesecloth whenever wanted. Cautiously strain the bone stock into it. Dispose of the spent pieces of bone and vegetables.

8. Cool the bone stock and store. Set up an ice shower by either filling a sink or bowl with cold water and ice and set the pot of stock inside

the ice shower. Mix routinely until the stock is cooled to about 50°F, around 15 minutes. Move the stock to sealed shut holders or containers. Refrigerate or freeze.

Moderate Cooker Instructions

9. Preheat the oven to 400°F and wash the bones. Organize a rack in the oven and warmth to 400°F. Spot the bones in a colander, flush under cool water, and wipe off with paper towels.

10. Cook the bones for 30 minutes. Organize the bones in a solitary layer on a rimmed preparing sheet. Cook until brilliant earthy colored, around 30 minutes.

11. Cover the bones with 3 quarts cool water and the vinegar and rest for 30 minutes. Move the issues that remains to be worked out 6-quart or bigger lethargic cooker. Add the water and vinegar and mix to consolidate. Cover and let sit for 30 minutes.

12. Bring to a stew on the HIGH setting. Turn the sluggish cooker to the HIGH setting high and carry the stock blend to a stew.

13. Skim the stock for the main hour. Check the lethargic cooker periodically, skimming off any

froth that gathers on a superficial level the main hour and adding extra water on a case by case basis to keep the ingredients covered. Keep the stock at a low stew on HIGH for 24 hours.

14. Add the onions and carrots and cook for another 12 to 24 hours. Add the carrots and onions and keep on stewing on the HIGH setting for 12 to 24 hours more, adding more separated water depending on the situation to keep the bones covered. The stock is done when it is a rich brilliant earthy colored and the bones are self-destructing at the joints.

15. Strain the bone stock. At the point when the stock is done, strain and cool the bone stock as fast as could be expected. Set a sifter over an enormous pot or even a stand blender bowl and line it with cheesecloth whenever wanted. Cautiously strain the bone stock into it. Dispose of the spent pieces of bone and vegetables.

16. Cool the bone stock and store. Set up an ice shower by either filling a sink or bowl with cold water and ice and set the pot of stock inside the ice shower. Mix consistently until the stock

is cooled to about 50°F, around 15 minutes. Move the stock to impenetrable compartments or containers. Refrigerate or freeze.

Formula Notes

1. Bones for bone stock: You can utilize any blend of hamburger, pork, or chicken bones for making bone stock. Adding some substantial bones, similar to short ribs or ham bones, will make a more extravagant tasting stock; you can likewise utilize the meat from the bones in different dishes.

2. Separated water: We utilized sifted water for more impartial testing. On the off chance that you have incredible tasting tap or well water, don't hesitate to utilize it here. Water separated with a channel or spigot channel functions admirably; packaged sifted water isn't needed.

3. Putting away and warming: The stock can be refrigerated for as long as 5 days or frozen for as long as 3 months. To warm, spill out as much stock as you'd like and warm it delicately on the oven or in the microwave.

4. Diminishing bone stock for capacity: To save money on cooler space, you can stew the stock

over low warmth on the burner until it's decreased significantly. Keep it at an uncovered stew — you should consider just to be not many air pockets as it stews. Make a note on the cooler holder that the stock should be diminished with water prior to utilizing.

16. Goulash

Total: 45 min| Active: 15 min| Yield: 6 servings

Ingredients

- 1 tablespoon olive oil
- 1 medium yellow onion, diced
- 3 cloves garlic, minced
- 1 pound ground hamburger
- Genuine salt and newly ground dark pepper
- 1 teaspoon paprika
- 2 teaspoons Italian flavoring
- 1 tablespoon tomato glue
- One 15-ounce can diced tomatoes

- One 15-ounce would tomato be able to sauce
- 1 teaspoon Worcestershire sauce
- 1 cup low-sodium hamburger stock
- 8 ounces cavatappi pasta
- 4 ounces sharp Cheddar, destroyed on the enormous openings of a case grater (around 1 cup), in addition to additional for serving
- 2 tablespoons chopped new parsley, in addition to additional for serving

Directions:

1. Goulash
2. Warmth the olive oil in a Dutch oven or hefty lined pot over medium warmth. Add the onion and cook, mixing at times, until relaxed, around 5 minutes. Add the garlic and cook, mixing, until fragrant, around 1 moment.
3. Add the hamburger and cook, blending and separating the meat with a wooden spoon, until carmelized and not, at this point pink, around 8 minutes. Add 1 teaspoon salt, a couple of toils of pepper, the paprika, and Italian flavoring to the hamburger and mix to consolidate. Cook, blending, until the paprika starts to toast and get fragrant, around 1 moment. Mix the tomato glue into the

hamburger combination to cover, at that point cook until the glue thickens and develops in shading, around 2 minutes.

4. Add the diced tomatoes, pureed tomatoes, Worcestershire and hamburger stock to the meat combination and mix, scraping up any carmelized bits from the lower part of the pot, to consolidate. Heat the blend to the point of boiling over medium warmth. Diminish the warmth to medium low and add the cavatappi. Cook, blending sporadically, until the pasta is still somewhat firm, 8 to 10 minutes.

17. Tomato-Braised Lentils with Broccoli Rabe

Total: 35 mins| Servings: 4

INGREDIENTS

- 4 tablespoons extra-virgin olive oil, isolated
- 1 medium onion (or shallots), finely chopped
- 1 clove garlic, minced
- 1/2 cups green French lentils
- 1 tablespoon tomato glue
- 3 cups stock (chicken or vegetable), in addition to some extra if necessary
- 1 enormous pack (or 2 little bundles) broccoli rabe
- 1 clove garlic, sliced

- 1 huge tomato, chopped
- 1/2 cup weighty cream
- 1 to 2 tablespoons margarine
- Modest bunch new basil leaves, generally torn
- Salt and pepper to taste.

Guidelines

1. Warmth two tablespoons of the olive oil in a weighty lined pot. Sweat the onions over low warmth for around 8 minutes until clear, preparing with salt and pepper. Add the minced garlic and cook one more moment. Add the lentils, tomato glue and a sprinkle of the stock. Increment warmth to medium and mix sometimes until stock has been retained. Keep adding stock and mixing every so often until the lentils are simply delicate, around 30 minutes.

2. Then, carry a different pot of water to bubble and set up a huge ice shower. Drop the broccoli rabe in the bubbling water and cook for 1 to 2 minutes. Eliminate with utensils and quickly place into ice shower until cool. Channel and wipe off. In a different dish or skillet, heat the excess 2 tablespoons of olive

oil. Add the sliced garlic clove and the broccoli rabe. Season with salt and pepper and sauté for 2 to 3 minutes.

3. Add the chopped tomato to the lentils and cook for 2 to 3 minutes. Add the cream and margarine, and taste for preparing when warm. Mix in the basil leaves; at that point serve promptly with the sautéed broccoli rabe on top.

18. Easy French Ratatouille

YIELD: Serves 8, Makes about 2 quarts | PREP TIME: 20 minutes | COOK TIME: 1 hour 5 minutes to 2 hours 15 minutes

INGREDIENTS

- 5 tablespoons olive oil, partitioned, in addition to additional for serving
- 1/2 pounds eggplant (1 enormous), huge dice
- Genuine salt
- Newly ground dark pepper

- 1/2 pounds zucchini or summer squash (3 to 4 medium squash), enormous dice
- 1 medium yellow onion, diced
- 2 cloves garlic, minced
- 2 branches new thyme
- 1 sound leaf
- 1 pound tomatoes (3 to 4 medium), enormous dice
- 1 enormous ringer pepper, huge dice
- 1/4 cup inexactly pressed new basil leaves, meagerly sliced, in addition to additional for serving

Guidelines

1. Warmth 2 tablespoons of the oil in a huge Dutch oven or substantial lined pot over medium-high warmth until sparkling. Add the eggplant, season liberally with salt and pepper, and cook, mixing once in a while, until sautéed in spots, around 2 minutes. Move to an enormous bowl.
2. Add 2 tablespoons of the oil to the pot. Add the zucchini, season liberally with salt and pepper, and cook, blending at times, until sautéed in

spots, around 2 minutes. Move to the bowl with the eggplant.

3. Diminish the warmth to medium. Add the leftover 1 tablespoon oil and the onion, season with salt and pepper, and cook, blending sporadically, until mollified and simply starting to brown, 6 to 8 minutes. Add the garlic, thyme, and narrows leaf and cook until fragrant, around 30 seconds. Add the tomatoes and ringer peppers. Add the saved eggplant and zucchini and tenderly mix to consolidate.

4. Bring to a stew, at that point turn down the warmth to medium-low. Stew, blending incidentally, for at any rate 20 minutes or up to 1/2 hours. A more limited cooking time will leave the vegetables in bigger, more particular pieces; longer cooking times will separate the vegetables into a luxurious stew.

5. Eliminate the straight leaf and thyme branches. Not long prior to serving, mix in the basil. Taste and season with salt and pepper on a case by case basis. Serve, sprinkling each presenting with more basil and showering with more olive oil.

Formula Notes

1. Making a bigger group: This formula can be multiplied and adjusted to utilize whatever vegetables you have.

2. Flavor additional items: For something other than what's expected, take a stab at adding a tablespoon of smoked paprika, a touch of red pepper drops, 1/4 cup of red wine, or a sprinkle of vinegar to the ratatouille.

3. Capacity: Leftovers can be put away in an impermeable holder in the cooler for as long as 5 days.

Conclusion

I would like to thank you for choosing this book. It contains recipes which are healthy and can easily be made in the Dutch oven. Hope these will help you in making dishes easily using a Dutch oven. Prepare at home and appreciate along with your family members.

 I wish you all good luck!

CPSIA information can be obtained
at www.ICGtesting.com
Printed in the USA
BVHW091526270521
608293BV00004B/1088